lania

PURPLE LEAVES, RED CHERRIES
A Gift for Mothers with Short Stories, Journal & Toolkit

Created and Edited by Tania Elfersy & Andrea Katzman

Illustrations by Nomi Melul Ohad

Flower Cap Press

Providence, Rhode Island

For more stories and toolkit ideas, visit our website and forum at:
www.purpleleavesredcherries.com

Merchandise with artwork from this book is available at:
www.purpleleavesredcherries.com/shop

Quantity discounts and customized labels are available to companies and organizations.
For more information, contact the publisher: **info@flowercappress.com**

Purple Leaves, Red Cherries: A Gift for Mothers with Short Stories, Journal & Toolkit

Published by:
Flower Cap Press
68 Dorrance Street, No. 303, Providence, RI 02903
info@flowercappress.com

Front cover and illustrations by Nomi Melul Ohad
www.purpleleavesredcherries.com/nomi

Visual concept and design by TitanBrandWise.com

First edition 2011
ISBN: 978-0-9829759-2-3
Printed in Israel

*Dedicated with love
to our children*

Table of Contents

A Gift 7

Preface: Inspired by a Goddess 8

Introduction: Disruptive Wonder 11

Our Contributors 14

Explorations: The Stories

In the Beginning

Transformed 18

Since the Beginning of Time 19

Fractions 20

Memory 21

Boundaries and Balance

Nature's Call 26

Beyond the Drops 27

Mother Time 28

A Piece of Me 29

Body

Love Affair 34

Getting it Right 35

Kegels 36

Down on the Floor 37

Who I Was, Who I Am

Defining Me 42

New Worlds 43

Something to Fix 44

Shift 45

Love

Mama 50

Room for Love 51

What I've Learned 52

We Match! 53

[In]Sanity

The Next Day 58

Dark Chocolate 59

Up in the Air 60

Detox 61

Relationships

Dirty Dishes 66

Holly 67

From the Deep End 68

Sandwiched 69

Difficult Days

That Mother in the Park 74

Awake 75

Precious Produce 76

Rocking 77

Work

Just a Mom 82

Out of My Life 83

The Power of Pee 84

Hi-Tech Mom 85

Sex

Curvaceous Power 90

Torn Apart 91

Want 92

Job Done 93

What is a Good Mother? Expectations

Confessions 98

The Bottle 99

Leaving Home 100

Hard Act to Follow 101

Wise Women

Sky High 106

Always 107

She Said 108

Family 109

Discoveries: Journal & Toolkit

Journal

How to Create Your Own Stories 115

Mothers' Toolkit

Declaration of Mother's Rights 158

Help Always Welcome 160

Five-Minute Wonders 162

Trade for Sanity 164

Rice-Paper Therapy 166

Today I Am Grateful 167

Quote Décor 168

Red Cherry Moments 170

Acknowledgements 173

Permissions 174

Join Us Online 175

A Gift

A Gift

For New Mothers and All Mothers

Welcome to the World of Purple Leaves, Red Cherries.

A world that celebrates your life as a mother.

With
Purple Leaves
Pages that invite you to reflect on the complexities of motherhood, inspire you with the words of other mothers and encourage you to create your own stories.

And with
Red Cherries
Moments of enlightenment that surface as you examine how motherhood flows through your life.

A gift to celebrate motherhood in a special way.

Tania Elfersy and Andrea Katzman

www.purpleleavesredcherries.com

Isis with infant Horus

Inspired by a Goddess

by Tania Elfersy

While holding my baby I came across a picture of Isis, the Egyptian goddess of motherhood and fertility. She was holding her son Horus. I was enthralled.

Isis once represented an ideal mother but to me, sitting alone with my baby, she reminded me of that most obvious of notions – that there have always been mothers.

Here was an ancient statue of a woman holding her baby like I was holding mine. Okay, I don't wear a headdress, but fashion aside, I saw myself reflected in her image. It reminded me of the mantra I would whisper to myself when I was having a hard mothering day – think how many mothers there have been throughout history and remember, your mom did it, your grandmothers did it (even in much tougher times) . . . and you can do it too!

Looking at Isis had inspired me by giving historical weight to the everyday tasks of motherhood. So I got to thinking, mostly in my shower – my "room of one's own" (where else do I get a peaceful moment by myself?) – that it would be wonderful to package a picture of Isis and other inspirational items as a gift for new mothers. A thoughtful, meaningful gift – so much more helpful than anti stretch mark cream! Since let's face it, being a mother (especially a new one) can sometimes keep you climbing up and down that ladder of insanity and wouldn't it be great if we mothers could have an easier time of it?

I thought there must be a way to embrace new mothers and make them feel like they are not alone; and there must be a way to provide mothers with an accessible outlet for creativity and expression, because these aspects of our core identity are so easily put aside when our lives are overwhelmed with the care of young children, often causing us to lose ourselves.

Excited by these ideas, I emailed my dear friend Andrea, co-creator of this book. Andrea is the woman in my life who, no matter how stuck I've felt when grappling with issues of motherhood, has always offered wise words that have made me feel better and less alone. So when she said that she loved the idea, we began working on the project together. And from the sighting of a goddess, *Purple Leaves, Red Cherries* was born.

Disruptive Wonder
by Tania Elfersy & Andrea Katzman

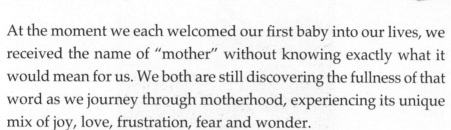

At the moment we each welcomed our first baby into our lives, we received the name of "mother" without knowing exactly what it would mean for us. We both are still discovering the fullness of that word as we journey through motherhood, experiencing its unique mix of joy, love, frustration, fear and wonder.

Mothering is so often invisible; we rarely noticed it before we ourselves became mothers. As we cared for our infants, motherhood began its slow and quiet course. Its effects trickled in between the cracks of our lives and flowed into underground reservoirs – occasionally creating a flash-flood, which always left its mark.

Looking back, we now understand that becoming a mother required a radical reinvention; we not only held a new baby, we owned a new identity. Motherhood demanded that we change in complex ways; no part of our lives was left untouched. We slowly redefined who we were – to ourselves and to others.

Today, as we share memories with each other, we realize that early on, we had few opportunities to reflect on what motherhood meant to us. We spent any spare reading time educating ourselves about child development and the impact of mothering on our children – on their self-esteem, their learning, their relationships, their ability to become well-adjusted adults. Yet we read very little about the impact of mothering on our self-esteem, our careers, our relationships and our ability to remain well-adjusted adults.

Our primary concern so often had been to be a "good" mother with happy children, which often led us to fixate on the "best" routes of parenting. That left little room for us to talk openly about the disruption motherhood brought to our lives as we entered a different mindset from that of our pre-mother selves.

Researchers tell us what we ourselves have observed: motherhood can be hard on women. One study concluded that half of all women with children under five regularly experience intense emotional distress.[1] Talking to other mothers, we quickly uncovered discontent on many levels. Yet we should not just sit back and assume this has to be the case.

We believe in the power of mothers connecting and sharing their experiences. We believe we can regain control of our lives before we feel washed away. We believe in the importance of realistic self-expectations and expressions of gratitude. With these beliefs, we have created *Purple Leaves, Red Cherries*.

Within this book you will find places to reflect, express, share and connect. We've included the voices of other mothers – 48 short stories, divided into 12 sections. As you journey through motherhood, we hope you will reread these stories and uncover new and different "red cherry" moments in each woman's tale. Mothering in the twenty-first century can sometimes feel lonely, but we hope that these voices remind you that as a mother, you are not alone.

In addition, we've created a hands-on Toolkit containing practical techniques to help you engage creatively in mothering. We've also included plenty of journal space throughout the book. We hope the stories, the Toolkit and the journal will help you to develop a more intimate and fulfilling understanding of your own experiences of motherhood.

This book is NOT another thing you "have" to do or complete. Instead, it is (we hope!) a source of inspiration, a safe space to express your feelings and a resource for preserving sanity and promoting happiness.

There is no timetable or required reading; feel free to dip in and dip out.

Enjoy your explorations and discoveries. Enjoy *your* purple leaves and red cherries.

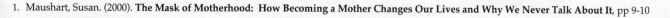

1. Maushart, Susan. (2000). **The Mask of Motherhood: How Becoming a Mother Changes Our Lives and Why We Never Talk About It**, pp 9-10

Our Contributors

Our contributors hail from three continents, raise their children within a variety of family structures and reflect a diversity of identities, backgrounds, livelihoods and attitudes toward motherhood.

Each story reflects the contributor's personal experiences. Not every tale of motherhood has been told in this book and we encourage you to write your own.

We are grateful to our contributors who found precious time in their busy lives to write their stories – each one in 140 words or less. We thank them for their courage, honesty and willingness to share.

Our contributors include:

Ann Ebner

Aviva Mishmari

Daphna Bahat

Dasee Berkowitz

Dina Kraft

Elizabeth H A Bollt

Hannah Rendell

Heidi Goodman

Jamie Faith Woods

Jo Frankel

Julie Rahav

Karen Welser

Kathryn Satterfield

Laliv Hadar

Leslie Jacobson-Cohen

Lisa Moss

Lisa Sacks

Liselle Terret

Mallory Serebin Jacobs

Natalie C

Nomi Melul Ohad

Pamela Romny Levanos

Renee Himelhoch Chemel

Sabrina Coletta Paradis

Sarah Ebner

Sharyn Brooks Katzman

Shlomit Gilony Barak

Susan Elfersy

Victoria Penny

In addition, a number of contributors wish to remain anonymous.

EXPLORATIONS: THE STORIES

Transformed

The day arrived. I had been consumed by work throughout my pregnancy and met my last deadline just before labor. I still couldn't believe that a baby would come out of me.

I wasn't ready.

And then I held Maya for the first time. Euphoria swept through me and left me breathless.

As I drew her close to my breast, the exhaustion of labor, the intense pain, my aching, bleeding body no longer mattered.

When we returned home I felt it was all a dream. I kept getting out of my bed to look at Maya asleep in her crib, wanting to make sure she was real.

The elation was more powerful than I could ever have imagined. I had become a mother and was transformed.

Natalie, mother of 3

Since the Beginning of Time

Nine months pregnant, I stomped out of the middle of a nursing seminar.

"I just can't sit and listen to this anymore," I said to my husband. "How hard could it be? Women have been breastfeeding since the beginning of time!"

Three weeks later, I was crying in my pediatrician's waiting room as I prepared to tell him I just couldn't breastfeed anymore.

No sleep. Huge cuts on my nipples. Latching. Un-latching. Re-latching. Lubricating. Walking around the house topless.

The baby, the pediatrician reported, was gaining nicely and was fine.

"But," I whimpered, "I am not."

Liz, mother of 3

Fractions

The lack of sleep completely overwhelmed me.

I felt tortured being awoken again and again just as I submerged into deep sleep. Mini cat naps became my excuses for sleep but they could not heal the all-over body exhaustion.

My baby completely controlled my schedule and I felt helpless. I couldn't fix it.

Desperate, I began recording the nap schedule, adding up the fractions of time to make it seem like some semblance of sleep. I thought I might feel better if I could convince myself that I had actually slept part of the night before.

It was only when my second child was born that I relinquished control over the sleep schedule. I accepted the fact that one day I would sleep again. . . . One day . . . .

Laliv, mother of 2

Memory

I had always imagined I would look back on the birth of my children and recall joy. But when my twin girls were born it was the scariest experience of my life.

My girls came far too soon, nearly three months early. None of us were prepared, especially them.

Forced out of my unconscious body, their first weeks of life were spent in incubators surrounded by medical teams, monitors and machinery.

The day I was discharged from the hospital I left not with a bundle of babies, but a boxed electric breast pump. For years that memory made me choke.

But now, eleven years later, I no longer see two tiny fragile girls, but two strong, charming, loving, intelligent individuals.

Finally, the way they came into this world is no longer relevant.

Jo F, mother of 3

My beginnings

Boundaries
and Balance

Nature's Call

I had to pee.

But once again I was lying on my bed nursing my voracious son. He never seemed to stop nursing and crying.

I couldn't figure out how to get to the bathroom with an eight-pound baby attached to my breast. I began sobbing.

"I have to pee," I cried. My husband responded with a clarity bred by a full night's sleep: "Just put him down and go!"

Why did it never occur to me that I could actually put down my baby and go to the bathroom?

Lisa M, mother of 3

Beyond the Drops

I was induced five weeks early. My baby arrived, but not my milk, not for a long time. Then it came at a dribble.

My son, Yan, became a "formula baby" and had no interest in learning to nurse. "Breast is best!" cried the experts, my friends and my family.

I was stressed.

I went to the best doctor in the field who gave me pills and advice and reinforced the benefits of breast.

For weeks I pumped and pumped. It hurt and took hours to get a few drops.

Finally I decided to give up and reclaim my sore nipples. What a relief to admit that breastfeeding wasn't working for Yan and me.

Heidi, mother of 1

Mother Time

I waited 45 years for the birth day. In an instant, I lost time as I knew it and a new world of time began to unfold.

My time was no longer my own.

Ten minutes alone in the shower or a solitary fifteen-minute walk for frozen yogurt became cherished luxuries.

What used to take ten minutes now took a whole day. An hour-long job became a week. A day-long project took a month.

I learned that time sitting and holding my child was as precious to me as being productive in my studio.

Mother time is often quiet, sometimes boring and frequently seen as unproductive.

Yet it is the most valuable gift I offer my child.

Mallory, mother of 1

A Piece of Me

I often feel as if I'm being pulled apart.

Each one of them wants a piece of me for something different at exactly the same time.

I don't even get to pee and take off my shoes, let alone grab a quick bite to eat in peace.

Don't they see that I need a few minutes to regroup?

I adore my kids, but I just don't have the ability to give each one ALL of me, ALL at the same time.

Not after a ten-hour day in the office. And really – I hate to admit it – at this moment, I am not that interested!

Jo F, mother of 3

Finding my balance

Body

Love Affair

In my twenties, I loved my breasts.

When I became pregnant a decade later, the love affair ended. The unimaginable swelling in pregnancy was followed by the rock-hard burn as my milk came in.

"Frozen peas," recommended the preternaturally calm woman from La Leche League. "Make it stop!" I cried in rage, bra wide open, nipples on fire, clutching tubes of lanolin.

Gradually breastfeeding became easier and I appreciated my breasts differently. Not just playthings: life-force!

When my daughter stopped nursing, it saddened me. I not only lost the daily intimate moments we had shared, I now had limp balloons where once were juicy peaches.

Luckily, modern bra technologies and helpful clerks have restored my shape, at least with my clothes on. And naked, at certain angles with dim light and squinty eyes, I imagine a return to perky glory.

Lisa S, mother of 2

Getting it Right

Despite my buoyant boobs, firm skin and flat stomach, I was filled with insecurity. During sex I was concerned about getting it right.

Then came the moment I was naked on all fours, grunting and pushing out my first baby. And my husband was right there watching. How could I be self-conscious about my body again?

In pregnancy, birth and mothering I have learned to let go and strive for happiness, not perfection. These lessons have been imprinted on my body and I have taken them into the bedroom.

My body has displayed tenacity and power to withstand expansion, birth and contraction. Motherhood has left its physical marks and given me body-confidence.

When intimate with my husband, I am free to lose myself in the moment. I just like my body better.

And go figure . . . so does he.

Andrea, mother of 2

Kegels

I can't use tampons anymore.

There are times (like in line at the supermarket) when the tampon will suddenly move down and I'll be stuck with something hanging out of my vagina.

After three vaginal births, my muscles down there have gone weak on me.

Is it not enough that my gravity-driven breasts have also shrunk to a former teenage size? That my tummy resembles a contour map of the Himalayas and that the veins in my legs have gone public?

Can I wear any of my new attributes with pride?

Mother of three with smaller breasts, bumpy tummy, decorated legs and can't-hold-a-tampon vagina!

Ah . . . mother of three. I'll forget the rest for now and think of my three little darlings. And maybe one day, I'll remember to do my Kegels.

Lillian, mother of 3

Down on the Floor

I'm hitting 40. My knees hurt a bit and my back aches.

When my five-year-old wants to play a game with me, I beg him to sit at the table, civilized, on a chair.

"No," he says, "we have to sit on the floor!"

So with creaking bones, I lower my body down and we begin to play. We chat, laugh, sing and make up new rules as we go. He takes several turns in a row, thinking I don't remember that he rolled last or turned over ten cards at a time. His legs are crossed, mine sprawled. We are level, eye-to-eye, on the same playing field.

These are the best times and I remember them well, when I begged my Dad to sit on the floor and play with me – his bones creaking as he lowered himself down.

Renee, mother of 2

Reflections of my body

Who I Was,
Who I Am

Defining Me

I was pushing my new baby in her pram, noticing the gazes of people walking past us in the street. How irritating, I thought, that they assumed I was "just" a mother.

I said to myself (and secretly to them), "In fact I am so much more than that. I shouldn't be defined by this tiny child."

Then I went out by myself pram-less for the first time. No one glanced at me and I felt irrationally upset. I thought, "I've got a baby. I'm not just a person walking down the street. I'm a mother too!"

And I realized this was it. I was forever both. I would forever feel that pull, the tension between the woman I am and the mother I had become.

Sarah, mother of 2

New Worlds

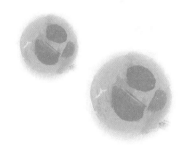

My son's world inspires me.

I am comforted by the protected space I have created for him. I am calmed by the sweet music I play at bedtime and energized by his colorful room.

His world encourages me to create a smaller world for myself too.

"The world is your oyster" attitude of my pre-childbearing years often left me wracked with anxiety that I was never doing enough.

I am still drawn to the world of people and ideas that extend beyond the confines of my home. Yet I know that my most profound connection is with the child sitting next to me.

Having a child anchors me.

Dasee, mother of 2

Something to Fix

After years of living alone, I was experienced at fixing things around the home. When I met my husband, I already had the power drill and well-stocked toolbox.

Then I became pregnant. I stopped climbing ladders, carrying heavy loads and avoided even vaguely toxic materials. My husband picked up the slack and slowly the pattern stuck.

Today I am a mom who rarely opens the toolbox, changes a bulb or fixes the toys. I even avoid taking out the trash. I'm an at-home mom with more than enough at-home responsibilities.

And my kids know it.

They know who to approach if something needs fixing and it ain't me.

It's a division of labor along traditional gender lines that leaves me unsettled.

Tania, mother of 3

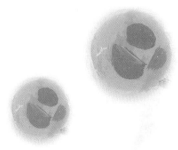

Shift

I'm so tired of my son – and myself – right now.

Something is missing from my life. I think it's creativity. I used to spend hours writing poetry, making collages, drawing comics, sculpting . . . .

Since I became a mother, my mental activity has been reduced to reading, internet and TV. I can't find the energy to do anything else. I feel like my son is growing up in a void – he's not being exposed to anything of the former me.

It's time for me to get creative again and in a way that he can join me. Maybe that will break my fatigue and relieve my frustration.

For now, emptiness is eating me up and it's about to creep into him as well. That can't be good.

How long does it take, being a mom? When is my shift over?

Aviva, mother of 2

I was, I am

Love

Mama

I come from the black hole of motherlessness, having lost my own mother at the tender age of 2 years, 9 months. I say it this way because every month, every moment with and without her has made a difference in my life.

In the darkness, I never imagined the great light that would come when I would one day hold my own beautiful baby. She entered my world and her tiny hands changed my life forever.

I often find myself confused about what I am doing that is meaningful in this world. But at three in the morning, when she is at my breast, I sink down into the scent of her perfect-pure babyness, and find peace.

Mama, she says softly, and I say yes, I am here.

Julie, mother of 2

Room for Love

It took a long time for us to become parents.

We went through cycle after cycle of failed IVF before I finally got pregnant. When our precious daughter was born eight-and-a-half months later, it felt like no mother on earth had ever loved her child more than I loved mine.

I would have died for her and I would have died without her.

When I became pregnant with her twin siblings a few years later, I was terrified. How could I possibly love one, let alone two babies, as much as I loved her?

But my heart has expanded – doubled, tripled and quadrupled in size as each of my children stirs up a different love.

How could I even begin to measure?

Emily, mother of 3

What I've Learned

I've learned to ignore developmental charts; still, I occasionally lapse into reading what "typical" kids do, and when.

Jaden isn't typical. He has a rare genetic disorder with no name. "We don't know what this means for your son," the geneticist said. "He could be anywhere from mildly to severely delayed."

The doctors had no prescription to give, simply: "Go home and love your son." I went numb.

Time passes, dreams fade – others take their place. Jaden smiles; he giggles; he crawls.

At 2½ Jaden walks unsteadily. He doesn't talk. But his face lights up when he sees me; he throws his arms around my neck to hug me. At night he tucks his body into mine. Warm and sleepy, he looks up, touches my face, smiles brightly.

Time passes, dreams fade – others take their place.

Kathy, mother of 1

We Match!

My husband and I have three children. Our first two we call "home-grown" – biologically ours, they look startlingly like us.

Our third child was adopted from across the seas. Her skin is a different color from mine. Her thick black hair falls in luxurious waves, while mine curls up tight.

Now three years old, she says to me, "I love you, Mama," and I tell her I love her also.

She says, "We're exactly the same. We both have two eyes. And a nose, and a chin, and cheeks . . . ."

She goes on to name our bodies, identifying part for part, until she gets to her favorite line:

"And we both love each other. We match!"

Karen, mother of 3

My loves

[In] Sanity

The Next Day

I've felt like throwing my baby out the window.

I didn't do it.

I called a friend, or handed the baby to someone else, or put him in his crib while I collected myself, even if he was still screaming. I made a cup of tea and then picked him up again and we cried together.

There was always hope that the next day he might cry a little less; that I might cry a little less.

It didn't make me a bad mom, that out-the-window feeling. I suspect many moms feel that way sometimes.

Kris, mother of 3

Dark Chocolate

When the most sophisticated thing I've done all week is eat dark chocolate; when piles of dirty laundry and unfolded clean laundry have become sites of volcanic activity; when once again I can't find anything to wear because even though it's winter outside, it's all four seasons in my closet; when the puzzle pieces are really missing; when I realize the only book I've finished in the last six months is one with 32 pages:

When all this happens, I might just get lucky and capture a sight of all three of my children laughing and playing together.

And I know I need to dive deep into that happiness, let it soak through my skin, because it is with them there, not here, that I want to be.

Tania, mother of 3

Up in the Air

I've been down on the ground looking up, waiting for life to fall on my head.

Things have been tough lately and I've been depressed.

Everything – our finances, the cleaning, the laundry, our sex life – seems to be up in the air.

Scott is three months old; Keith, seventeen months. Two babies are a challenge and "me" doesn't always fit into the equation.

But I'm slowly finding the time to get back into shape mentally and physically.

I'm trying to figure it all out.

Liz, mother of 3

Detox

When we arrived home with our third child, serenity filled the air. My partner and I understood the new rhythm and gracefully measured out between us the tasks of parenting three.

In the weeks following the birth of our first two children we had existed in temporarily altered states. Arguing in ways we never had before, we reached new relationship lows.

Back then, we struggled under the influence of that insane post-natal cocktail – mutual fatigue, my raging hormones, the intensity of the new mother-baby bond, his increased sense of responsibility and the action replay of me birthing our child – all shaken, not stirred.

But weeks had passed since the birth of our third child. With parenting wisdom and our new abilities to instantly detox, we had coped.

Sanity would prevail.

Salena, mother of 3

My sanity

Relationships

Dirty Dishes

When he returns from work he asks, "How was your day?"

He looks worried. He is wondering when the explosion is going to hit him.

Earlier I had called him at work, sobbing, because the baby wouldn't stop crying. He answered, "What do you expect me to do from here?"

Now he tells me, "I had a busy day and everyone heard you were crying. What happened? Why are you so sad?"

All day long, feelings of anger, frustration and guilt swirled around in my head. Now they are piled up like the dirty dishes in the sink.

I hand him the baby.

There's a mess at home. My day was filled with endless little tasks. I'm exhausted and empty from it all despite the huge love for my baby.

How can I explain the "nothing" that happened?

Nomi, mother of 2

Holly

When I first became a mom, I was surrounded by "child-free" friends. I loved them, but they no longer understood me.

I needed mom friends.

But how could I find the time and energy to meet anyone new when I could hardly function due to sleep deprivation and my daily saga of "the frustrating adventures in nursing?"

I was getting desperate.

So I emailed Holly, a woman I had met in birthing class. Having begun casually, the emails quickly evolved into intimate missives. We realized we were both confronting so many shared new experiences – and none of them pretty!

We started meeting weekly, commiserating over the trials and tribulations we faced as mothers. Holly validated my feelings in ways no book or family member ever could.

Six years later, I can't imagine life without Holly, my dear mom friend.

Jamie Faith, mother of 2

From the Deep End

Suddenly immersed in the world of mothering, I was flailing in the deep end of the pool. My husband waded in the shallow water.

He wasn't moving toward me. I wasn't calling for him.

We could no longer relate to each other's daily experiences. We tried to reach out to each other, but exhaustion and stress prevented our reunion.

Still, there was a long history of love. We assured each other that our distance wouldn't last.

With time, we reconnected.

Perhaps we would never understand each other's first experiences of parenting. But holding his hand, I left the deep end and together we built a marriage that was more flexible, supportive and forgiving.

We became better and more loving partners than ever before.

Sophia, mother of 2

Sandwiched

I am 41, raising two beautiful girls, trying to be the best mom and wife I can while watching my aging parents deteriorate.

My girls need me.

In them, I see promise and opportunity, hope and joy. They open my heart and heal my soul. My daughters look at me with admiration and a silent plea: "Mommy, keep me safe, love me, accept me, be with me."

My mom and dad – the two people who loved me first – also need me.

They are becoming tired and often are not well. They are more dependent and less confident. My parents once protected me. Now they add their silent plea: "Leslie, it is your turn. Here, have the reins. Take them. Please."

I am a girl, a woman, a daughter, a wife and a mother.

God, please keep me strong.

Leslie, mother of 2

My relationships

Difficult Days

That Mother in the Park

I was a new mother of two, breastfeeding my baby on a park bench as my two-year-old son played nearby. It felt good. I felt in control . . . until my son started playing recklessly on a slide.

Tensions rose.

My son was refusing to listen to me and my baby was becoming increasingly upset from the interruptions in her nursing.

Then it happened.

I became that mother in the park no mother wants to be. I yanked my baby off my boob and placed her screaming in her pram. I yanked my son off the slide and placed him screaming over my shoulder. Then, with two shrieking children and my milk dripping, I walked home.

Once home I nursed my baby and calmed my son. I was just me again, regular me. The moment had passed.

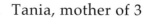

Tania, mother of 3

Awake

A baby wails, the same baby I could have sworn I just got down to sleep. Again.

Is that a herd of water buffalos stampeding into the room or is it just my darling firstborn knocking into furniture, reaching her hands into the crib and giving her baby brother a good morning thwack?

Escalation ensues. More thwacks, a bite to the baby's toe.

As humans we are wired to protect our young. But what happens when our young turn on each other?

What happens is another "difficult day." One in which I could swear some superior version of me as a mom floats in a parallel universe.

I desperately want to reach her through the ether. Have her whisper me her secrets.

Dina, mother of 2

Precious Produce

Unable to breastfeed, I expressed milk for my firstborn.

Five, six, seven times a day, my pump milked me. Each time immobilized, I watched the drops slowly fill a bottle. A labor of love without the warmth of my baby.

I became a pumping pro, but it was beginning to milk the life out of me. After six months, and with a precious three weeks' supply of my milk lovingly frozen, I packed up my pump.

Days later when the compressor on our nearly new freezer went to compressor heaven, it took my milk with it too.

Six years later it still brings tears to my eyes as I recall pouring bag after bag of thawed and spoiled breast milk down the sink.

Emily, mother of 3

Rocking

You lie content in your crib.

I'm rocking, trying to comfort my whole self. With tears running down my face, I'm agonizing:

"Why did you choose me? What if I'm not good enough? What if I'm not enough? What if I fail?"

My soul aches, I'm so alone. How did this happen? Why me? Why you?

You are six months old . . . .

One year old . . . .

How can you already be two?

I look back at the years and breathe deeply.

We can do this. We are going to be okay.

Leslie, mother of 2

My difficult days

Work

Just a Mom

Mothering has to be the only job in the world where even as I gain more experience, I cannot call myself an expert.

Just when I feel like I'm getting the hang of it all, the goalposts change and I enter a new phase with my children. The physical and mental demands are unpredictable and often overwhelming.

At work, my days are so much calmer. I'm a professional with a proven record. As I gain experience I become more skilled and competent. I know when I've done a good job and benefit from constructive feedback.

Motherhood means I often feel uncertain. I struggle to make do with the tools and knowledge I've picked up along the way.

I do the best job I can. But at home, I'm "just" a mom.

Jo K, mother of 2

Out of My Life

I was a criminal lawyer. My husband and I passed the bar the same year.

Ten years later, we had our first child. After my maternity leave, I returned to work and employed a nanny.

Every morning, I greeted the nanny. Every evening, I relieved her. Then, after putting my daughter to bed, I made food, tidied up and struggled to prepare my case for the next day.

I ran between home and court, working frantically in both arenas. My husband's work was sacrosanct. He carried on as if nothing had changed.

He never shopped, cooked, cleaned, unloaded the dishwasher or sorted laundry.

I was overloaded. I juggled my career with motherhood and failed.

After the birth of my second child, I gave up my practice at the bar. Now I am retraining to be a teacher. And divorcing my husband.

Victoria, mother of 2

The Power of Pee

My son wet his bed this morning. While he was still half asleep, I changed his diaper, put him into fresh pajamas and changed his sheets. I did this in complete darkness so as not to wake the whole house.

Did I mention I was wearing a brand new black business suit and three-inch heels?

All day at work I felt like saying to my co-workers, "Think that meeting was bad? Did you change cold, peed-on sheets and a wet child this morning at 4am? Did ya, huh?"

There are days in my life that are so hard I can't even think about showering. Or days when laundry feels like the enemy. But then there are days where getting through the sheer grossness of motherhood makes me feel more powerful than any new suit alone could.

Sabrina, mother of 2

Hi-Tech Mom

I work full-time.

My motto is: I give the best hugs and kisses, but doing housework doesn't make me a better mother.

When my husband and I first became parents, we were also beginning our careers. Our salaries were low. Most of our income went toward childcare and domestic help, which allowed us to advance in our professions and raise our five children together.

I've always dedicated evenings and weekends to my kids. This quality time remains the best defense against any lingering feelings of guilt.

Sometimes, after a long day, I find myself cradling the phone while comforting a baby with one hand and answering emails with the other. I feel weighed down.

But I continue to multitask, fly around the world, outsource what I can and give the best hugs and kisses to my children.

Daphna, mother of 5

My work

Sex

Curvaceous Power

He had always said he liked larger women. I had a curvaceous body while pregnant that I kept after birth and he wouldn't touch me.

He complained about the baby – her crying, her noisy nursing, the space we took up in bed. All of it disturbed him.

He thought I had become dull.

"What happened to my girlfriend?" he asked.

Initiating intimacy, I unleashed my passion. We made deep, lustful love twice. Afterwards, he said he wished it had never happened. He hated losing control.

I could no longer reach out to him. I cuddled my baby in our bed and gazed at her as she suckled on my breast. I felt empowered.

A mother's body.

My power. His lack of it.

Anna, mother of 2

Torn Apart

During the birth of my first child, I tore inside and was cut outside. It took them a long time to stitch me up.

At three months my partner and I tried having sex. We tried again at six months. Both times it hurt horribly.

I thought perhaps the physical pain reflected my exhausted mental state. I couldn't imagine a time when sex would replenish me. I had disconnected from desire.

Then, around a year after birth, I decided to find the source of the pain. Three medical examinations finally revealed that I had been sewn up wrong, so I was re-cut and re-sewn.

Eventually I healed, but the challenge was to enjoy sex again. I was still traumatized by memories of pain.

With time, my longing for pleasure overcame my fear. I was willing to share my body again.

Carli, mother of 2

Want

I want my husband to want me.

I want to please him – my dear, patient love.

Oh, and I know that I'll lie in the afterglow and ask, "Why can't we do this more often?"

But the thought of it. It's so exhausting. I want a cup of tea, damn it!

What has become of me again? After each birth that wilderness of sexlessness expands and I walk through it ever slower, carrying an extra bag of fatigue.

I need to start ovulating. I remember that gives me energy.

Then I'll get back in the driver's seat and he'll enjoy the view.

And we'll discover each other anew.

Sunita, mother of 3

Job Done

It used to be that I couldn't fall asleep without sex. Three children later, there is a distinct lack of action in our bedroom.

Our everyday lives are drying out the passion.

Okay, there are times (normally on vacation) when our libidos are amazingly reawakened. But then routine takes over again – work, laundry, cooking, cleaning, shopping – and who has time to think of sex?

And then, there were those times when as already exhausted parents we decided to have another child. We had a mutual understanding that fatigue was no excuse. Night after night we would get to work until the job was done.

My husband says it's lucky that we need to have sex to get pregnant. I don't recall procreating being much fun – could I even call it sex?

I miss having time and space for passion.

Shlomit, mother of 3

My sexual journey

What is a Good Mother? Expectations

Confessions

Before I had my first child, I read all the books. The path to "good" mothering was clear: no crying-it-out, no bottles, no inconsistencies . . . .

Those were the theories. Here are my confessions:

Sometimes, when my baby was screaming, I would put him in his bed and shut the door so I couldn't hear his cries. I would have a drink of water, get myself back together and only then return to his room.

Sometimes, when my baby woke up hungry in the night, I would let my husband feed him formula so I could continue sleeping.

I love my little boy more than anything in the world, but there are times I break my own rules.

I realize now that those beliefs I once held so dear are not sacred; staying sane requires compromise and flexibility.

Hannah, mother of 1

The Bottle

I hated formula.

I hated companies that made formula. I fought with medical professionals who suggested using formula. At every visit, I cleared out all the formula pamphlets from our pediatrician's waiting room.

My own children nursed well and long. I was full of self-righteous pride.

Then post-partum depression enveloped a close friend. She wasn't sleeping or eating. She was often in tears and felt hopeless. She was wary about telling me that breastfeeding overwhelmed her, fearing my disapproval.

I was devastated.

My ideals had blinded me from the complexities of motherhood and from my friend's pain.

While my friend slept, went to therapy and slowly recovered, I bought formula. I mixed it, and while holding her sweet baby, I gratefully fed him the bottle.

Andrea, mother of 2

Leaving Home

Crying, I held four-month-old Micah in my arms, warm, soft and sleeping. He was my third child, but I wouldn't be an at-home mom anymore.

I had decided to return to teaching. He would go to daycare.

I had joyfully stayed home with my two older children until they were school age. When I was pregnant with Micah, I assumed that I would stay home with him also.

But things had changed. I had changed.

I cried and kissed his face and gazed at him some more. I hoped that it would be alright, and that he would be alright.

But I knew that this was the choice I had to make.

Pam, mother of 3

Hard Act to Follow

My mother is a great mother.

It's hard to live up to someone like my mom, a person so wise, sensible, giving and kind. I try, but I don't think I manage it.

How can I emulate someone who's on such a high pedestal? I attempt to raise my children the way she raised us, teaching good manners, respect for others and compassion for the world beyond.

But sometimes I feel they would have been luckier to have had my mom as their mom. I'm not as calm, not as wise and not as brilliant.

I glow inwardly when my parents praise my parenting or compliment my children. It makes me feel that I'm on the right track.

Still, I think that my mom is a very hard act to follow. I don't think that feeling will ever change.

Sarah, mother of 2

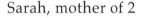

My expectations

Wise Women

Sky High

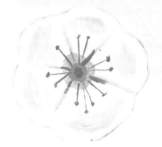

Over forty years ago when my first child was born, I knew almost nothing about babies and there were few books to turn to.

Women stayed in the hospital for ten days after giving birth and feeding the baby was strictly regulated – a set number of minutes every four hours.

I was determined to breastfeed but my baby kept falling asleep at feeding time and one nurse complained that I was taking too long. She insisted I use a bottle.

I didn't listen. Then a really supportive nurse appeared. She got the experienced mother in the next bed to show me how she breastfed her baby.

When the babies were weighed at five days, most had lost some birth weight. But my little one had actually put on a fraction.

My confidence leapt sky high and we never looked back.

Susan, mother of 3, grandmother of 8

Always

Sobbing and gulping, I pushed my week-old daughter around the circle of sidewalk in front of our first rented home. I wailed to my puzzled husband, "Is it always going to be like this?"

The new mother sleep-fog, my sore body, the flakes on my baby's scalp – you name it – I was the designated family worrier. I staggered under the crushing burden of "what-ifs?"

Forty years later, I recognize the truth of it.

It always will be like this: the knock-me-to-my-knees overwhelming love for my child, the frustration that I can't hand over a perfect and happy life to her, the petty and large concerns that still buzz about.

And the incomparable, heart-stopping joy of then and now and always being my daughter's mother.

Sharyn, mother of 2, grandmother of 5

She Said

The thing about a mother's advice is that it often comes unannounced and is rarely well labeled.

Patrick Preston was our newspaper boy. According to my mother, he was using his route money to put himself through a private high school. One day, my mother put her mink over her velour housecoat and took a cab over to Patrick's school.

She told the headmaster that Patrick was her paperboy and that her paper had been delivered every day without fail. Then she paid his tuition for the rest of the year.

When I asked her why she did it, she said, "Because I can. Sometimes it's nice just to be nice."

My mother died when I was young, long before she could impart much advice. But to me her lasting advice is:

Be nice just because you can.

Sabrina, mother of 2

Family

As a young mother I didn't feel very wise. Everything was new, especially the dependence of small children.

I understood my role was to structure the home. I wanted my children to feel safe and loved. I wanted to establish boundaries and instill in them values, so that they could later contribute to the wider society.

As a grandmother I have grown wiser from experience.

I have adapted to my children making their own way, not always to my liking. I recognize that each generation faces new pressures.

As I listen to each individual in my family, I hope I can hear them. I offer advice when asked, support when needed and provide unconditional love.

And I bestow continuity. The repository of family history and traditions are within me.

I am the conduit from past to future generations.

Ann, mother of 3, grandmother of 7

Wise women in my life

Journal

How to Create Your Own Stories

Writing in a journal can help clarify thoughts, soothe troubled feelings, point to constructive action and re-energize spirits. But sometimes when faced with an empty journal page, it can feel overwhelming. Where do I start? What do I write about?

Try constructing your own stories with these creative aids:

Use a writing prompt – A word or sentence that stokes your imagination and triggers a story. Here are some examples:

- Beginnings
- Transformation
- Sleep
- Memories
- Courage
- Love
- Achievements

- What do you think is beautiful?
- What three words best describe you right now?
- When do you feel lonely?
- When was the last time you cried and why?
- When do you feel happy?
- When do you feel most grateful?

Compose a letter – To your mother, partner or someone you love. Send it or not, as you wish.

Write freely – Set aside ten minutes to write in your journal - non-stop. Don't worry about grammar, spelling, word choice or flow.

Illustrate your feelings – In addition to words, use color, line and form to express your emotions.

Trust yourself – Believe that your feelings and experiences (everyday ones as well as momentous ones) are important and deserve space in your journal.

Be honest – Don't self-edit. Your journal is a treasured, confidential space. Enjoy the raw written word.

Mothers' Toolkit

Tools to survive and thrive in motherhood

. . . although sometimes just surviving is good enough!

*D*eclaration of Mother's Rights

In the beginning, it can often feel like there is no routine and that our needs are forgotten. But if we long for some quiet time with a cup of coffee in the morning, fifteen minutes to read a book in the afternoon or a short walk in the evening, we can prioritize it. These were not unreasonable demands before we were mothers and they shouldn't be now.

Spend time thinking about something you can't (or won't) live without. Write your own Declaration of Mother's Rights.

Andrea's right: To nurse at night without feeling lonely.

During the day I dreaded the too quiet nights. We didn't have a TV – even though it was 1998! I wanted just a little one in our bedroom, so we bought a cheap TV and put it on the dresser. We didn't get cable, but I found one news channel whose cheerful and energetic newscasters kept me company through the night as I nursed my baby.

Tania's right: To begin every day by taking a shower.

In order to function, I needed to shower EVERY DAY. It became my husband's responsibility to make sure this happened. No matter how early he needed to leave for work in the morning, he had to schedule taking care of the baby for 15 minutes while I had time to shower and prepare myself to greet the day.

Declaration of Mother's Rights

When in the course of human events, one becomes a mother . . . . We hold these truths to be self-evident, that all women are created equal, that they are endowed with certain unalienable Rights, that among these are Life, Liberty and the pursuit of Happiness.

That to secure these rights, this mother requires:

1.

2.

3.

4.

5.

$\mathcal{H}$elp Always Welcome

When a new baby arrives we all need support. Visitors who come to our home often will ask, "What can I do to help?"

Consider copying the suggested tasks from the box onto paper slips. Leave the slips in your own **Helping Box** by the front door for visitors to pick up. Feel free to add your own tasks that you would like help with.

Even if creating a **Helping Box** is not suitable in your home, writing down the tasks that you would like help with can remind you that help is always welcome.

Wash/dry/
fold/put
away laundry
(choose one or more)

Make me food

Look after
the baby
while I shower

Change the
bed sheets

Make me a cup
of tea (and hold
the baby while
I drink it)

Vacuum

Wash dishes

Make me laugh

Feed me dark
chocolate

Take out the trash

Five-Minute Wonders

MAKE IT!
CREATE IT!
DO IT!

Do you feel like you've been busy all day, but have accomplished next-to-nothing?

Your baby has just gone to sleep and you have a list of things to do. But do you feel sure that the moment you get down to work, your baby will suddenly wake up and cry for you?

Would you like to create something special for yourself and complete it in just a few minutes?

Open your Toolkit envelope and try one of our Five-Minute Wonders!*

1. Brighten your bedside table with a paper bird-of-paradise flower
2. Refresh yourself with a facial
3. Smooth your hands with a hand scrub
4. Sing and dance to your favorite song from your teenage years (hairbrush mic optional)
5. Make a soothing herbal soak for your bath
6. Reenergize yourself with a delicious smoothie
7. Decorate your home with a *Purple Leaves, Red Cherries* mobile
8. Email your mom-friends and invite them and their babies to a *Purple Leaves, Red Cherries* party
9. Write freely – without interruption – in your *Purple Leaves, Red Cherries* Journal

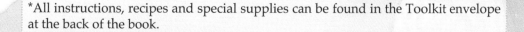

*All instructions, recipes and special supplies can be found in the Toolkit envelope at the back of the book.

Trade for Sanity

Sometimes when we're struggling, there may be a way to juggle our budgets and life choices to preserve our sanity.

Look at your budget, your choices and your circumstances. Use your imagination. Make a list of things you need and a list of things you already have – and are willing to give up. See how you can make a trade.

Tania's Trade for Sanity:
With two children and a third planned, I needed help close by more than anything else. I traded living in a city neighborhood I loved for living around the corner from my supportive parents-in-law (in their aging, less hip neighborhood).

Andrea's Trade for Sanity:
I wanted to work two mornings a week but a babysitter was too expensive. I found a group of moms who also needed childcare and we set up and ran our own playgroup. I traded being with my two children for going out to work and, every two weeks, babysitting for six boisterous kids (and cleaning up the wreckage afterwards!)

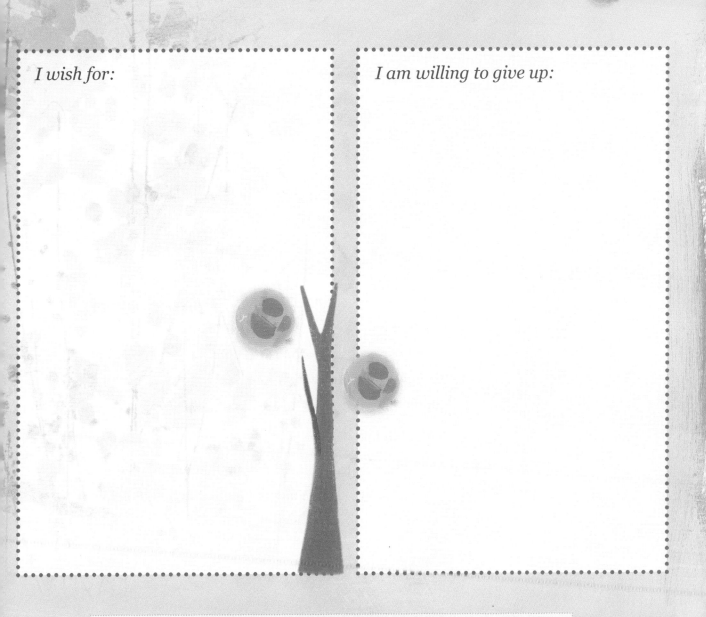

I wish for:

I am willing to give up:

For additional Trade for Sanity examples go to the Inspire Me section of our website: **www.purpleleavesredcherries.com/inspireme**

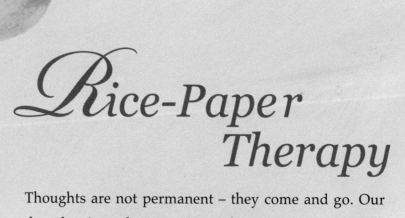

Rice-Paper Therapy

Thoughts are not permanent – they come and go. Our thoughts do not have to define who we are, nor must they dictate what we do.

We can acknowledge them and witness them float away.

Write down a troubling or painful thought on a piece of rice-paper.* Place it in a bowl of warm water and watch the thought slowly dissolve.

166

*Rice-paper is included in the Toolkit envelope at the back of the book.

Today I Am Grateful

Write down the everyday wonders in your life for which you are grateful.

Today I am grateful for:

Quote Décor

Post the Toolkit quote slips* around your home. Let them inspire you when you open the fridge, look in the mirror, change a diaper or at any other time.

Create additional personalized quote slips by printing out the quote slip template available in the Inspire Me section of our website:

www.purpleleavesredcherries.com/inspireme

*Included in the Toolkit envelope at the back of the book.

"There is a tremendous amount of learning that takes place in the first year of your baby's life; the baby learns a lot, too."

Debra Gilbert Rosenberg

"Having a baby is a terrible drain on the resources. . . . He's not bringing in any money on his own. Lately he sits around in his underwear all day playing the harmonica."

Anne Lamott

"I had crossed over to a strange new world, a world where another person's life literally depended on me. . . . And this sense of being in a strange land was all the more jarring since, of course, I hadn't left home."

Andrea Buchanan

"And eventually being perfect became like carrying a backpack filled with bricks every single day. . . . What is really hard, and really amazing, is giving up on being perfect and beginning the work of becoming yourself."

Anna Quindlen

"Mothering is perhaps the greatest story never written. The journey to motherhood is an odyssey of epic proportions, and every woman who undertakes it a hero."

Susan Maushart

"Real mothers know that mothering is not a reflexive behavior but an acquired art."

Natalie Angier

My Red Cherry Moments:

Red Cherry Moments

Stick the red cherry stickers*
next to text in this book that has
enlightened and empowered you.

*Included in the Toolkit envelope at the back of the book.

Acknowledgements

We thank those whose work you see in this book: our contributors who graciously shared their stories; our dear, loving and generous artist, Nomi Melul Ohad, whose inspiring artwork so beautifully decorates the book and alights its spirit; and the wonderfully gifted tribe that is Titan, whose design transformed our manuscript into a treasured gift, with special mention to Merav, Michal and Liri for their tremendous talents and enthusiasm.

We thank our perceptive proofreader (and queen of the comma), Sara K. Eisen; and we thank those who took *Purple Leaves*, *Red Cherries* to the internet: EG Studio and our savvy social media strategist, Debra Askanase.

We thank all those whose generous contributions may be unapparent to the reader but whose efforts enabled this book to come to fruition: Sharyn Brooks Katzman and David Katzman, Andrea's parents and true editors extraordinaires – we are indebted to their wise words, guidance and generosity; Susan and Armand Elfersy, Tania's parents, who encouraged us every step of the way with love and wisdom; Hannah and Moshe Hamami whose continuous support and delicious supply of home-cooked food has been enjoyed by all; our early readers Ariel, Dalia, Heidi, Jennie and Jodie who took time away from caring for their sweet babies to provide us with precious feedback; and our friends and families for their practical help, suggestions and professional expertise, with special mention to Jude, Pam and the Elfersy, Jacobson and Katzman families.

We thank our husbands, Erez and Steven. Creating this book enabled us to pursue our passions and make a dream come true. Without their extraordinary love, infinite patience, continuous encouragement and belief in our vision, we would not have been able to accomplish what we did. And we are so grateful to our children, Amittai, Ayala, Erella, Ariela and Elieza. They remained amazingly patient as we read, wrote, edited, emailed and talked while promising that we'd be done in "only five more minutes . . . ." They help make us the moms we are and have brought more joy and love into our lives than we ever thought possible.

Permissions

We thank the following authors for inspiring us on our journey and for providing permission to use their quotes:

Natalie Angier, **Woman: An Intimate Geography.** Published by Houghton Mifflin (1999). Copyright © by Natalie Angier. Quote reprinted by permission of author.

Andrea J. Buchanan, **Mother Shock: Loving Every (Other) Minute of It.** Published by Seal Press, an imprint of the Perseus Books Group (April 2003). Copyright © by Andrea J. Buchanan. Quote reprinted by permission of author.

Anne Lamott, **Operating Instructions: A Journal of My Son's First Year**. Published by Pantheon Books, a division of Random House, Inc. (1993). Copyright © by Anne Lamott. Quote reprinted by permission of author.

Susan Maushart, **The Mask of Motherhood: How Becoming a Mother Changes Our Lives and Why We Never Talk About It.** Published by Penguin Books (2000). Copyright © by Susan Maushart. Quote reprinted by permission of author.

Anna Quindlen, **Being Perfect.** Published by Random House, Inc. (April, 2005). Copyright © by Anna Quindlen. Quote reprinted by permission of author.

Debra Gilbert Rosenberg, **The New Mom's Companion: Care for Yourself While You Care for Your Newborn.** Published by Sourcebooks, Inc. (April 2003). Copyright © by Debra Gilbert Rosenberg. Quote reprinted by permission of author.

Join Us Online

The world of *Purple Leaves, Red Cherries* continues on our website:
www.purpleleavesredcherries.com

On our website, visit our **Forum** to:

- Join discussions about the texts that appear in this book.
- Post your own stories, Five-Minute Wonders, Trade for Sanity, Quote Décor additions and Red Cherry Moments.
- Read and comment on the postings of other readers.

www.purpleleavesredcherries.com/forum

Discover more Mothers' Toolkit tips plus the best of the forum postings in the Inspire Me section of our website:
www.purpleleavesredcherries.com/inspireme

We look forward to connecting with you there.

Love the illustrations in this book?

Visit our *Purple Leaves, Red Cherries* shop:
www.purpleleavesredcherries.com/shop

Send a free *Purple Leaves, Red Cherries* e-card:
www.purpleleavesredcherries.com/ecards